Written on the Leaves

Written on the Leaves

Haiku Poems & Linocut Prints

Jenna Weston

Written on the Leaves
Copyright © Jenna Weston, 2016

All rights reserved. This book may not be reproduced in whole or in part, in any form without written permission of the author.

ISBN-13: 978-1532942044
ISBN: 1532942044

Illustrations: Jenna Weston
Book Design: Melanie A. Wegner

This book is dedicated to my mother, Jackie Stanley, who taught me to notice the little things in nature, and to all those who are helping to preserve our endangered natural world.

Go to the pine if you want to learn about the pine, or to the bamboo if you want to learn about the bamboo. Your poetry issues of its own accord when you and the object have become one — when you have plunged deep enough into the object to see something like a hidden glimmering there.

Matsuo Basho
Japanese Haiku Poet (1644-1694)

Table of Contents

Introduction 1

Spring.. 5

Summer 23

Autumn 39

Winter. 55

Acknowledgements 70

About the Author.. 71

Introduction

FORM

You may notice that the haiku in this book are not written in the 5-7-5 syllable count that is traditional to Japanese haiku. This is because English and Japanese have such different grammatical devices. Adhering strictly to a 17-syllable rule can produce awkwardness in English haiku—such as padding with extra words or, alternately, truncating phrases in order to "fit" into a defined form.

I do however, strive to retain several core haiku principles in my poems:

- Making a connection between nature and human nature
- Writing three short lines; the middle line usually being the longer one
- Linking a fragment and a phrase
- Showing a single moment, using the present tense
- Evoking a specific time and place
- Using concrete images rather than abstractions or commentary
- Choosing the fewest words necessary to convey the essence of an experience

PLACE

Poetry is, at its root, often autobiographical, and the haiku poems I write are no exception. They reflect the different geographical locations where I have lived over the years. Pieces of Michigan, Missouri, North Carolina and Florida are brought together in this North American-based collection of haiku. A good portion of my poems reference the rural environments where I've made my home, while a smaller number speak of urban themes experienced during the few times I lived in a city.

"ECOLOGICAL" HAIKU

Since its beginning centuries ago, the haiku poem has changed many times in response to the times and places where it has been written. It is my belief that this poetic form must continue to evolve if it is to remain vital and relevant. It would follow that today's haiku must reflect the natural world as it exists now: one that still holds much beauty, but that is also being destroyed at an alarming rate.

Nature today is a far cry from what it was centuries ago in the time of the famous Japanese haiku master Basho. To continue to write about the natural world only in an idealized fashion is, in my opinion, to do a disservice to the haiku principle of showing the-moment-as-it-is. This is why some of the haiku I write depict damaged environments. I'm not trying to be depressing. I don't seek out ecological devastation, but neither do I turn away when I encounter it.

Traditionally, haiku is not supposed to have an agenda or be "political," but in these precarious times simply speaking the truth can seem radical. I do want my poetry to affect my readers—in ways that draw them closer to nature while also showing how vulnerable and in need of protection our natural world has become.

Spring

A long black skirt –
the edge of the storm
dragging its hem

                    Laundry on the clothesline
                    drips beneath grey clouds –
                    a second rinse cycle

Drops of water
roll down the spring leaf
onto my tongue

Walking a dirt road
beneath the moon yesterday's rain –
potholes filled with light

After the flood
vivisected creek banks,
veins exposed

Eroded hillside –
sycamore roots groping
space

Water rushes down drains –
city creeks run vertically,
nature turned sideways

Street puddle –
under the oil slick
tadpoles wriggle

Spring thaw –
the landfill sprouting
shards of glass

Leaves moving
in a morning breeze –
green prayer flags

The window frames white
twice – pear blossoms
through curtain lace

Under live oaks
scarves hang on the clothesline –
Spanish moss

Too much shade –
only three peonies open
but... those three peonies!

Pink begonia
petals float in the water
of the cat's dish

Overpowering
April's air – too-sweet flowers?
scented dryer sheets

Butterfly ignoring
a bed of roses –
lands on this weed

Abandoned homestead –
what woman's daylily bulbs
still bloom here each spring?

Disappearing bees –
space around the blossoms
space where blossoms were

Closing the window
to muffle sounds of traffic –
bird song is muted too

In silence the heron
lifts one slow foot...sets it down –
walking meditation

Half-swallowed snake
tail tightening a noose
around the egret's pale neck

Existing because
a long-ago finch paused here –
this mulberry tree

Stuck in traffic –
a robin in the median
pulling worms

Road-killed skunks –
buzzards' return migration
is just in time!

A turtle saunters
across four lanes of highway –
what are the chances?

Strands of mane
from the curry comb
lining bird nests

Their thread
mending rips in earth's garment –
the unseen spinners

Summer

The sun casts a net
of light on the pool –
catches my attention

Out of touch I stand
under a waterfall pounding
sense back into me

Creekside boulder
upholstered with moss –
plush seating, but damp

Searching for the creek
afraid it has disappeared –
listen ... underground

Takes me to a time
before time – the smell
of the ocean

Broken beach glass,
waves blunting sharp edges –
your lies worn smooth

Seeing into them
I gather broken shells
leaving the perfect ones

Floating
in the round lake the sky
is a circle

Sunlit lake –
ripples shimmy across
the cottage ceiling

Fish dart to the surface –
concentric rings
targeting mayflies

Widening shoreline –
the egret's long neck curves
like a question mark

A broken road sign
by the dried-up lake –
Serena becomes Sere

Too upset about
the roadside trash to see
daisies growing there

Forest's frontline guards
keeping the two-leggeds out –
summer seed ticks

Morning stillness
before the heat
a pine needle drops

My pen's ink dry
grass crunches underfoot
this long drought

                              Cicada's shrill call –
                              acoustic thermometer
                              of the rising heat

Emerging here too –
cicadas in the city
louder than traffic

Sky-blue
butterflies circle
the cow dung

Between our faces
cutting through words in mid-
sentence -- hummingbird

Relentless whippoorwill
sending late night love letters
with repeated phrases

A plant near
the air conditioner –
leaves shiver through summer

Sitting down to lunch
irises on the table –
eyes eating flowers

Ladybug travels
the garden bucket's
endless rim

Early summer –
picking unexpected beans
into my T-shirt

So glad the spade missed!
it looked like a potato
that lumpy brown toad

The longing
to pick an unripe peach –
this day's fruit: patience

Purple fingers
squeeze the last drops from summer
making wild grape jam

Autumn

Early morning
packing your lunch for work
I slip in a love note

Waiting
for the season to change
to sleep again

Empty hands,
pockets are only holes –
what can be held?

Deleting your name
from my address book
it is finally real

Alone by the lake
noticing each duck
has a mate

Under a night sky
the half-feral cat comes near –
purrs with my weeping

Letting the pear
ripen too long –
slicing into regret

Autumn morning
lake steams in chill air –
still water still warm

White egret's flight
between grey lake and grey sky –
antidepressant

A white spot
on the dock marks
the heron's rest stop

On the tin roof
time ticks erratically –
acorns dropping

Poems fall from trees –
pages from a loose-leaf book
turned by wind

Unbalanced
the tipped cup spills acid rain –
hope drops tree by tree

All logged but saplings –
will they ever mature
without their elders?

Sapling
beside the steep hiking trail –
bark worn smooth, hand-high

A dead tree leaning
against another dead tree –
don't sit in that spot!

On a sandy path
not stepping on ant hills –
mindfulness

Leaf-covered
graveyard of abandoned cars –
Autumn is rusting

On the busy street
exquisite silence
between passing cars

Fragile white heads –
dandelions await the breeze
not quite ready to let go

Children in rows –
outside the classroom
scattered wild flowers

Invisible play –
the wind? or recent children?
empty swings moving

Taking the trash
to the curb – a glimpse
of the neighbors

Loud daybreak meeting
argumentative voices –
the crows, caucusing

Holding the flashlight
to pick all the green tomatoes –
first frost predicted tonight

                Chastened by the frost,
                even harsh poison ivy's
                leaves blush pink

November wind chimes –
leaves clinking on the tree
each one wrapped in ice

Winter

Time-capsule –
layered beneath asphalt
a dirt road, a deer path

Patches of snow?
the woods are spotted with white –
plastic grocery bags

On this clear-cut land
nothing is left unbroken –
limbs, trunks, roots, our hearts

Sunset's red jet trails
cross over empty fields
X-ing out the sky

Gazing at the night sky –
what phase is the moon tonight?
the streetlight is always full

Hard to read
pages obscured by
a demanding cat

Burrowing
into a book I pull
the cover over me

Sun through window blinds –
strips of light cross
the sleeping cat's stripes

Her meow garbled
through a mouth full
of mouse

        Waking before dawn
        to the morning blessing –
        soft paw on my cheek

Meditation –
right in the middle the dog
wanting to go out

How few ounces
of leaping squirrel it takes
to sway an oak limb

Winter's chill –
the heron folds itself
to half its height

Singing within
a cathedral of cliffs–
coyotes' midnight mass

Full-moon city night
sirens howling past the door –
urban coyotes

December dusk
clouds heavy with unshed snow
a lone goose flies south

Between two panes
a smudge of moth
wing dust

Ionic scrollwork
architecture of winter's frieze –
spiral frost flowers

Trees like inked lines,
calligraphy of vines
on winter's rice paper

Slicing the light
into wedges –
palmetto's long knives

Live oak –
within its twisted limbs
autobiography

Catalpa tree –
wind plays percussion
on dry seed pods

Two girl friends laughing:
one pretty, the other not –
both beautiful

Senses reeling
we stumble from the gallery –
now the whole street is art!

Cut off in childhood
creativity itches –
a phantom limb

After the last guest –
putting away
the leftovers

So different
from not speaking –
shared silence

ACKNOWLEDGEMENTS

I am very grateful for the incisive critiques of my poems by haiku luminary Jim Kacian. His feedback helped me become a better haiku writer.

Judith Armstrong's long-time encouragement of my art and writing, and Melanie Wegner's graphic expertise contributed greatly to making this book a reality. Both are also dear friends.

I deeply appreciate the numerous ways my spouse, Worth Bodie lovingly supports me and my work.

Many thanks to the members of my writers groups in Asheville, NC and Gainesville, FL, and to all the amazing women who have continued to make the Womonwrites Conference happen for the past 40 years.

ABOUT THE AUTHOR:

Jenna Weston was born in Michigan and homesteaded for 22 years in the Missouri Ozarks. A deep connection with the natural world is evident in her poetry and art. She now lives on a small lake in North Florida and is dedicated to helping protect the springs and aquifers in the region.

www.jennaweston.com

Printed in Great
Britain
by Amazon